Amleth, Prince of Denmark

Saxo Grammaticus

Amleth, Prince of Denmark

Table of Contents

Amleth, Prince of Denmark From the Gesta Danorum of Saxo Grammaticus

translated by Oliver Elton

Horwendil, King of Denmark, married Gurutha, the daughter of Rorik, and she bore him a son, whom they named Amleth. Horwendil's good fortune stung his brother Feng with jealousy, so that the latter resolved treacherously to waylay his brother, thus showing that goodness is not safe even from those of a man's own house. And behold when a chance came to murder him, his bloody hand sated the deadly passion of his soul.

Then he took the wife of the brother he had butchered, capping unnatural murder with incest. For whoso yields to one iniquity, speedily falls an easier victim to the next, the first being an incentive to the second. Also the man veiled the monstrosity of his deed with such hardihood of cunning, that he made up a mock pretense of goodwill to excuse his crime, and glossed over fratricide with a show of righteousness. Gerutha, said he, though so gentle that she would do no man the slightest hurt, had been visited with her husband's extremest hate; and it was all to save her that he had slain his brother; for he thought it shameful that a lady so meek and unrancorous should suffer the heavy disdain of he husband. Nor did his smooth words fail in their intent; for at courts, where fools are sometimes favored and backbiters preferred, a lie lacks not credit. Nor did Feng keep from shameful embraces the hands that had slain a brother; pursuing with equal guilt both of his wicked and impious deeds.

Amleth beheld all this, but feared lest too shrewd a behavior might make his uncle suspect him. So he chose to feign dullness, and pretend an utter lack of wits. This cunning course not only concealed his intelligence but ensured his safety.

Amleth, Prince of Denmark

Every day he remained in his mother's house utterly listless and unclean, flinging himself on the ground and bespattering his person with foul and filthy dirt. His discolored face and visage smutched with slime denoted foolish and grotesque madness. All he said was of a piece with these follies; all he did savored of utter lethargy. In a word, you would not have thought him a man at all, but some absurd abortion due to a mad fit of destiny.

He used at times to sit over the fire, and, raking up the embers with his hands, to fashion wooden crooks, and harden them in the fire, shaping at their tips certain barbs, to make them hold more tightly to their fastenings. When asked what he was about, he said that he was preparing sharp javelins to avenge his father. This answer was not a little scoffed at, all men deriding his idle and ridiculous pursuit; but the thing helped his purpose afterwards. Now is was his craft in this matter that first awakened in the deeper observers a suspicion of his cunning. For his skill in a trifling art betokened the hidden talent of the craftsman; nor could they believe the spirit dull where the hand had acquired so cunning a workmanship. Lastly, he always watched with the most punctual care over his pile of stakes that he had pointed in the fire. Some people, therefore, declared that his mind was quick enough, and fancied that he only played the simpleton in order to hide his understanding, and veiled some deep purpose under a cunning feint.

His wiliness (said these) would be most readily detected, if a fair woman were put in his way in some secluded place, who would provoke his mind to the temptations of love; all man's natural temper being too blindly amorous to be artfully dissembled, and this passion being also too impetuous to be checked by cunning. Therefore, if his lethargy were feigned, he would seize the opportunity, and yield straightway to violent delights. Some men were commissioned to draw the young man in his rides into a remote part of the forest, and there assail him with a temptation of this nature. Among these chanced to be a foster–brother of Amleth, who had not ceased to have regard to their common nurture; and who esteemed his present orders less than the memory of their past fellowship. He attended Amleth among his appointed train, being anxious not to entrap, but to warn him; and was persuaded that he would suffer the worst if he showed the slightest glimpse of sound reason, and above all if he did the act of love openly. This was also plain enough to Amleth himself. For when he was bidden mount his horse, he deliberately set himself in such a fashion that he turned his back to the neck and faced about, fronting the tail; which he proceeded to encompass with the reins, just as if on that side he would check the horse in its furious pace. By this cunning thought he eluded the trick, and overcame the treachery of his uncle. The reinless steed galloping on, with the rider directing its tail, was ludicrous enough to behold.

Amleth went on, and a wolf crossed his path amid the thicket. When his companions told him that a young colt had met him, he retorted, that in Feng's stud there were too few of that kind fighting. This was a gentle but witty fashion of invoking a curse upon his uncle's riches. When they averred that he had given a cunning answer, he answered that he had spoken deliberately: for he was loath to be thought prone to lying about any matter, and wished to be held a stranger to falsehood; and accordingly he mingled craft and candor in such wise that, though his words did lack truth, yet there was nothing to betoken the truth and betray how far his keenness went.

Again, as he passed along the beach, his companions found the rudder of a ship which had been wrecked, and said they had discovered a huge knife. "This" said he, "was the right thing to carve such a huge ham;" by which he really meant the sea, to whose infinitude, he thought, this enormous rudder matched.

Also, as they passed the sandhills, and bade him look at the meal, meaning the sand, he replied that it had been ground small by the hoary tempests of the ocean. His companions praising his answer, he said that he had spoken it wittingly.

Then they purposely left him, that he might pluck up more courage to practice wantonness. The woman whom his uncle had dispatched met him in a dark spot, as though she had crossed him by chance; and he took her and would have ravished her, had not his foster-brother, by a secret device, given him an inkling of the trap. For this man, while pondering the fittest way to play privily the prompter's part, and forestall the young man's hazardous lewdness, found a straw on the ground and fastened it underneath the tail of a gadfly that was flying past; which he then drove towards the particular quarter where he knew Amleth to be: an act which served the unwary price exceedingly well. The token was interpreted as shrewdly as it had been sent. For Amleth saw the gadfly, espied with curiosity the straw which it wore embedded in its tail, and perceived that it was a secret warning to beware of treachery. Alarmed, scenting a trap, and fain to possess his desire in greater safety, he caught up the woman in his arms and dragged her off to a distant and impenetrable fen. Moreover, when they had lain together, he conjured her earnestly to disclose the matter to none, and the promise of silence was accorded as heartily as it was asked. For both of them had been under the same fostering in their childhood; and this early rearing in common had brought Amleth and the girl into great intimacy.

So, when he had returned home, they all jeeringly asked him whether he had given way to love, and he avowed that he had ravished the maid. When he was next asked where he did it, and what had been is pillow, he said that he had rested upon the hoof of a beast of burden, upon a cockscomb, and also upon a ceiling. For, when he was starting into temptation, he had gathered fragments of all these things, in order to avoid lying. And though his jest did not take aught of the truth out of the story, the answer was greeting with shouts of merriment from the bystanders.

The maiden, too, when questioned on the matter, declared that he had done no such thing; and her denial was the more readily credited when it was found that the escort had not witnessed the deed. Then he who had marked the gadfly in order to give a hint, wishing to show Amleth that to his trick he owed his salvation, observed that latterly he had been singly devoted to Amleth. The young man's reply was apt. Not to seem forgetful of his informant's service, he said that he had seen a certain thing bearing a straw flit by suddenly, wearing a stalk of chaff fixed on its hinder parts. The cleverness of this speech, which made the rest split with laughter, rejoiced the heart of Amleth's friend.

Thus all were worsted, and none could open the secret lock of the young man's wisdom.

But a friend of Feng, gifted more with assurance than judgment, declared that the unfathomable cunning of such a mind could not be detected by any vulgar plot, for the man's obstinacy was so great that it ought not to be assailed with any mild measures; there were many sides to his wiliness, and it ought not to be entrapped by any one method. Accordingly, said he, his own profounder acuteness had hit on a more delicate way, which was well fitted to be put in practice, and would effectually discover what they desired to know. Feng was purposely to absent himself, pretending affairs of great import. Amleth should be closeted alone with his mother in her chamber; but a man should first be commissioned to place himself in a concealed part of the room and listen heedfully to what they talked about. For if the son had any wits at all he would not hesitate to speak out in the hearing of his mother, or fear to trust himself to the fidelity of her who bore him. The speaker, loath to seem readier to devise than to carry out the plot, zealously proffered himself as the agent of the eavesdropping. Feng rejoiced at the scheme, and departed on pretense of a long journey. Now he who had given up this counsel repaired privily to the room where Amleth was shut up with his mother, and lay down skulking in the straw.

But Amleth had his antidote for the treachery. Afraid of being overheard by some eavesdropper, he at first resorted to his usual imbecile ways, and crowed like a noisy cock, beating his arms together to mimic the flapping of wings. Then he mounted the straw and began to swing his body and jump again and again, wishing to try if aught lurked there in hiding. Feeling a lump beneath his feet, he drove his sword into the spot, and impaled him who lay hid. Then he dragged him from his concealment and slew him. Then, cutting his body into morsels, he seethed it in boiling water, and flung it through the mouth of an open sewer for the swine to eat, bestrewing the stinking mire with his hapless limbs.

Having in this wise eluded the snare, he went back to the room. Then his mother set up a great wailing and began to lament her son's folly to his face; but he said: "Most infamous of women! dost thou seek with such lying lamentations to hide thy most heavy guilt? Wantoning like a harlot, thou hast entered a wicked and abominable state of wedlock, embracing with incestuous bosom thy husband's slayer, and wheedling with filthy lures of blandishment him who had slain the father of thy son. This, forsooth, is the way that the mares couple with the vanquishers of their mates; for brute beasts are naturally incited to pair indiscriminately; and it would seem that thou, like them, hast clean forgot thy first husband. As for me, not idly do I wear the mask of folly; for I doubt not that he who destroyed his brother will riot as ruthlessly in the blood of his kindred. Therefore it is better to choose the garb of dullness than that of sense, and to borrow some protection from a show of utter frenzy. Yet the passion to avenge my father still burns in my heart; but I am watching the chances, I await the fitting hour. There is a place for all things; against so merciless and dark a spirit must be used the deeper devices of the mind. And thou, who hadst been better employed in lamenting thine own disgrace, know it is superfluity to bewail my witlessness; thou shouldst weep for the blemish in thine own mind, not for that in another's. On the rest see thou keep silence." With such reproaches he rent the heart of his mother and redeemed her to walk in the ways of virtue; teaching her to set the fires of the past above the seductions of the present.

When Feng returned, nowhere could he find the man who had suggested the treacherous espial; he searched for him long and carefully, but none said they had seen him anywhere. Amleth, among others, was asked in jest if he had come on any trace of him, and replied that the man had gone to the sewer, but had fallen through its bottom and

5

been stifled by the floods of filth, and that he had then been devoured by the swine that came up all about that place. This speech was flouted by those who heard; for it seemed senseless, though really it expressly avowed the truth.

Feng now suspected that his stepson was certainly full of guile, and desired to make way with him, but durst not do the deed for fear of the displeasure, not only of Amleth's grandsire Rorik, but also of his own wife. So he thought that the King of Britain should be employed to slay him, so that another could do the deed, and he be able to feign innocence. Thus, desirous to hide his cruelty, he chose rather to besmirch his friend than to bring disgrace on his own head. Amleth, on departing, gave secret orders to his mother to hang the hall with knotted tapestry, and to perform pretended obsequies for him a year thence; promising that he would then return. Two retainers of Feng then accompanied him, bearing a letter graven on wood—a kind of letter enjoined the king of the Britons to put to death the youth who was sent over to him.

While they were reposing, Amleth searched their coffers, found the letter, and read the instructions therein. Whereupon he erased all the writing on the surface, substituted fresh characters, and so, changing the purport of the instructions, shifted his own doom upon his companions. Nor was he satisfied with removing from himself the sentence of death and passing the peril on to others, but added and entreaty that the King of Britain would grant his daughter in marriage to a youth of great judgment whom he was sending to him. Under this was falsely marked the signature of Feng.

Now when they had reached Britain, the envoys went to the king, and proffered him the letter which they supposed was an implement of destruction to one another, but which really betokened death to themselves. The king dissembled the truth, and entreated them hospitably and kindly. Then Amleth scouted all the splendor of the royal banquet like vulgar viands, and abstaining very strangely, rejected that plenteous feast, refraining from the drink even as from the banquet. All marveled that a youth and a foreigner should disdain the carefully–cooked dainties of the royal board and the luxurious banquet provided, as if it were some peasant's relish. So, when the revel broke up, and the king was dismissing his friends to rest, he had a man sent into the sleeping–room to listen secretly, in order that he might hear the midnight conversation of his guests.

Now, when Amleth's companions asked him why he had refrained from the feast of yestereve, as if it were poison, he answered that the bread was flecked with blood and

6

tainted; that there was a tang of iron in the liquor; while the meats of the feast reeked of the stench of a human carcass, and were infected by a kind of smack of the odor of the charnel. He further said that the king had the eyes of a slave, and that the queen had in three ways shown the behavior of a bondmaid. This he reviled with insulting invective not so much the feast as its givers. And presently his companions, taunting him with his old defect of wits, began to flout him with many saucy jeers, because he blamed and caviled at seemly and worthy things, and because he attacked thus ignobly and illustrious king and a lady of so refined a behavior, bespattering with the shamefullest abuse those who merited all praise.

All this the king heard from his retainer; and declared that he who could say such things had either more than mortal wisdom or more than mortal folly; in these few words fathoming the full depth of Amleth's penetration. Then he summoned his steward and asked him whence he had procured the bread. The steward declared that it had been made by the king's own baker. The king asked where the corn had grown of which it was made, and whether any sign was to be found there of human carnage? The other answered, that not far off was a field, covered with the ancient bones of slaughtered men, and still bearing plainly all the signs of ancient carnage; and that he had himself planted this field with grain in springtide, thinking it more fruitful than the rest, and hoping for plenteous abundance; and so, for aught he knew, the bread had caught some evil savor from this bloodshed.

The king, on hearing this, surmised that Amleth had spoken truly, and took the pains to learn also what had been the source of the lard. The other declared that his hogs had, through negligence, strayed from keeping, and battened on the rotten carcass of a robber, and that perchance their pork had thus come to have something of a corrupt smack.

The king, finding that Amleth's judgment was right in this thing also, asked of what liquor the steward had mixed the drink? Hearing that it had been brewed of water and meal, he had the spot of the spring pointed out to him, and set to digging deep down; and there he found, rusted away, several swords, the tang whereof it was thought had tainted the waters. Others relate that Amleth blamed the drink because, while quaffing it, he had detected some bees that had fed in the paunch of a dead man; and that the taint, which had formerly been imparted to the combs, had reappeared in the taste.

7

The king, seeing that Amleth had rightly given the causes of the taste he had found so faulty, and learning that the ignoble eyes wherewith Amleth had reproached him concerned some stain upon his birth, had a secret interview with his mother and asked her who his father had really been. She said she had submitted to no man but the king. But when he threatened that he would have the truth out of her by a trial, he was told that he was the offspring of a slave. By the evidence of the avowal thus extorted he understood the whole mystery of the reproach upon his origin. Abashed as he was with shame for his low estate, he was so ravished with the young man's cleverness, that he asked him why he had aspersed the queen with the reproach that she had demeaned herself like a slave? But while resenting that the courtliness of his wife had been accused in the midnight gossip of a guest, he found that her mother had been a bondmaid. For Amleth said he had noted in her three blemishes showing the demeanor of a slave; first, she had muffled her head in her mantle as bondmaids do; next, that she had gathered up her gown for walking; and thirdly, that she had first picked out with a splinter, and then chewed up the remnant of food that stuck in the crevices between her teeth. Further, he mentioned that the king's mother had been brought into slavery from captivity, lest she should seem servile only in her habits, yet not in her birth.

Then the king adored the wisdom of Amleth as though it were inspired, and gave him his daughter to wife; accepting his bare word as though it were a witness from the skies. Moreover, in order to fulfill the bidding of his friend, he hanged Amleth's companions on the morrow. Amleth, feigning offense, treated this piece of kindness as a grievance, and received from the king, as compensation, some gold, which he afterwards melted in the fire, and secretly caused to be poured into some hollowed sticks.

When he had passed a whole year with the king he obtained to make a journey, and returned to his own land, carrying away of all his princely wealth and state only the sticks which held the gold.

On reaching Jutland, he exchanged his present attire for his ancient demeanor, which he had adopted for righteous ends, purposely assuming an aspect of absurdity. Covered with filth, he entered the banquet–room where is own obsequies were being held, and struck all men utterly aghast, rumor having falsely noised abroad his death. At last terror melted into mirth, and the guests jeered and taunted one another, that he whose last rites they were celebrating as though he were dead, should appear in the flesh.

Amleth, Prince of Denmark

When he was asked concerning his comrades, he pointed to the sticks he was carrying, and said, "Here is both the one and the other." This he observed with equal truth and pleasantry; for his speech, though most thought it idle, yet departed not from the truth; for it pointed at the weregild of the slain as though it were themselves. Thereon, wishing to bring the company into a gayer mood, he joined the cupbearers, and diligently did the office of plying the drink.

Then, to prevent his loose dress hampering his walk, he girded his sword upon his side, and purposely drawing it several times, pricked his fingers with its point. The bystanders accordingly had both sword and scabbard riveted across with an iron nail.

Then, to smooth the way more safely to his plot, he went to the lords and plied them heavily with draught upon draught, and drenched them all so deep in wine, that their feet were made feeble with drunkenness, and they turned to rest within the palace, making their bed where they had reveled. Then he saw they were in a fit state for his plots, and thought that here was a chance offered to do his purpose. So he took out of his bosom the stakes he had long ago prepared, and went into the building, where the ground lay covered with the bodies of the nobles wheezing off their sleep and their debauch. Then, cutting away its supports, he brought down the hanging his mother had knitted, which covered the inner as well as the outer walls of the hall. This he flung upon the snorers, and then applying the crooked stakes, he knotted and bound them up in such insoluble intricacy, that not one of the men beneath, however hard he might struggle, could contrive to rise.

After this he set fire to the palace. The flames spread, scattering the conflagration far and wide. It enveloped the whole dwelling, destroyed the palace, and burnt them all while they were either buried in deep sleep of vainly striving to arise. Then he went to the chamber of Feng, who had before this been conducted by his train into his pavilion; plucked up a sword that chanced to be hanging to the bed, and planted his own in its place. Then, awakening his uncle, he told him that his nobles were perishing in the flames, and that Amleth was here, armed with his old crooks to help him, and thirsting to exact the vengeance, now long overdue, for his father's murder. Feng, on hearing this, leapt from his couch, but was cut down while, deprived of his own sword, he strove in vain to draw the strange one.

Amleth, Prince of Denmark

O valiant Amleth, and worthy of immortal fame, who being shrewdly armed with a feint of folly, covered a wisdom too high for human wit under a marvelous disguise of silliness! and not only found in his subtlety means to protect his own safety, but also by its guidance found opportunity to avenge his father. By this skillful defense of himself, and strenuous revenge for his parent, he has left it doubtful whether we are to think more of his wit or his bravery.

Amleth, when he had accomplished the slaughter of his stepfather, feared to expose his deed to the fickle judgment of his countrymen, and thought it well to lie in hiding till he had learnt what way the mob of the uncouth populace was tending. So the whole neighborhood, who had watched the blaze during the night, and in the morning desired to know the cause of the fire they had seen, perceived the royal palace fallen in ashes; and, on searching through its ruins, which were yet warm, found only some shapeless remains of burnt corpses. For the devouring flame had consumed everything so utterly, that not a single token was left to inform them of the cause of such a disaster. Also they saw the body of Feng lying pierced by the sword, amid his blood-stained raiment. Some were seized with open anger, others with grief, and some with secret delight. One party bewailed the death of their leader, the other gave thanks that the tyranny of the fratricide was now laid at rest. Thus the occurrence of the king's slaughter was greeted by the beholders with diverse minds.

Amleth, finding the people so quiet, made bold to leave his hiding. Summoning those in whom he knew the memory of his father to be fast-rooted, he went to the assembly and there made a speech after this manner:

> Nobles! Let not any who are troubled by the piteous end of Horwendil be troubled by the sight of this disaster before you: be not ye, I say, troubled, who have remained loyal to your king and duteous to your father. Behold the corpse, not of a prince, but of a fratricide. Indeed, it was a sorrier sight when ye saw our prince lying lamentably butchered by a most infamous fratricide—brother, let me not call him. With your own compassionating eyes ye have beheld the mangled limbs of Horwedil; they have seen his body done to death with many wounds. Surely that most abominable butcher only deprived his king of life that he might despoil his country of freedom! The hand that slew him made you slaves.

Amleth, Prince of Denmark

Who then so mad as to choose Feng the cruel before Horwendil the righteous?

Remember how benignantly Horwendil fostered you, how justly he dealt with you, how kindly he loved you. Remember how you lost the mildest of princes and justest of fathers, while in his place was put a tyrant and an assassin set up; how you rights were confiscated; how everything was plague–stricken; how the country was stained with infamies; how the yoke was planted on your necks, and how your free will was forfeited! And now all this is over; for ye see the criminal stifled in his own crimes, the slayer of his kin punished for his misdoings.

What man of but ordinary wit, beholding it, would account this kindness a wrong? What sane man could be sorry that the crime has recoiled upon the culprit? Who could lament the killing of a most savage executioner? or bewail the righteous death of most cruel despot?

Ye behold the doer of the deed; he is before you. Yea, I own that I have taken vengeance for my country and my father. Your hands were equally bound to the task which mine fulfilled. What it would have beseemed you to accomplish with me, I achieved alone. Nor has I any partner in so glorious a deed, or the service of any man to help me. Not that I forget that you would have helped this work, had I asked you; for doubtless you have remained loyal to your king and loving to your prince. But I chose that the wicked should be punished without imperiling you; I thought that others need not set their shoulders to the burden when I deemed mine strong enough to bear it. Therefore I consumed all the others to ashes, and left only the trunk of Feng for your hands to burn, so that on this at least you may wreak all your longing for a righteous vengeance.

Now haste up speedily, heap the pyre, burn up the body of the wicked, consume away his guilty limbs, scatter his sinful ashes, strew broadcast his ruthless dust: let no urn of barrow enclose the abominable remnants of his bones. Let no trace of his fratricide remain; let there be no spot in his own land for his tainted limbs; let no neighborhood suck infection from him; let not sea nor soil be defiled by harboring his accursed carcass. I have done the rest; this one loyal duty is left for you. These must be the tyrant's obsequies, this the funeral procession of the fratricide. It is not seemly that he who stripped his country of her freedom should have his ashes covered by his country's earth.

Besides, why tell again my own sorrows? Why count over my troubles? Why weave the thread of my miseries anew? Ye know them more fully than I myself. I, pursued to the death by my stepfather, scorned by my mother, spat upon by friends, have passed my years in pitiable wise, and my days in adversity; and my insecure life has teemed with fear and perils. In fine, I passed every season of my age wretchedly and in extreme calamity. Often in your secret murmurings together you have sighed over my lack of wits: there was none (you said) to avenge the father, none to punish the fratricide. And in this I found a secret testimony of your love; for I saw that the memory of the King's murder had no yet faded from your minds.

Whose breast is so hard that it can be softened by no fellow–feeling for what I have felt? Who is so stiff and stony, that he is swayed by no compassion for my griefs? Ye whose hands are clean of the blood of Horwendil, pity your fosterling, be moved by my calamities. Pity also my stricken mother, and rejoice with me that the infamy of her who was once your queen is quenched. For this weak woman had to bear a two–fold weight of ignominy, embracing one who was her husband's brother and murderer.

Therefore, to hide my purpose of revenge and to veil my wit, I counterfeited a listless bearing; I feigned dullness; I planned a stratagem; and now you can see with your own eyes whether it has succeeded, whether it has achieved its purpose to the full; I am content to leave you to judge so great a matter.

It is your turn: trample under foot the ashes of the murderer! Disdain the dust of him who slew his brother, and defiled his brother's queen with infamous desecration, who outraged his sovereign and treasonably assailed his majesty, who brought the sharpest tyranny upon you, stole your freedom, and crowned fratricide with incest. I have been the agent of this just vengeance; I have burned for this righteous retribution: uphold me with a high–born spirit; pay me the homage that you owe me; warm me with your kindly looks. It is I who have wiped off my country's shame; I who have quenched my mother's dishonor; I who have beaten back oppression; I who have put to death the murderer; I who have baffled the artful hand of my uncle with retorted arts.

Were he living, each new day would have multiplied his crimes. I resented the wrong done to father and to fatherland: I slew him who was governing you outrageously and more hardly than it beseemed men. Acknowledge my service, honor my wit, give me the throne if I have earned it; for you have in me one who has done you a mighty service, and who is no degenerate heir to his father's power; no fratricide, but the lawful successor to the throne; and a dutiful avenger of the crime of murder.

You have me to thank for the recovery of the blessings of freedom, for release from the power of him who vexed you, for relief from the oppressor's yoke, for the shaking off the sway of the murderer, for trampling the despot's scepter under foot. It is I who have stripped you of slavery, and clothed you with freedom; I have restored your height of fortune, and given you your glory back; I have deposed the despot and triumphed over the butcher. In your hands is the reward: you know what I have done for you: and from your righteousness I ask my wage.

Every heart had been moved while the young man thus spoke; he affected some to compassion, and some even to tears. When the lamentation ceased, he was appointed king by prompt general acclaim. For one and all rested the greatest hopes on his wisdom, since he had devised the whole of such an achievement with the deepest cunning, and accomplished it with the most astonishing contrivance. Many could have been seen marveling how he had concealed so subtle a plan over so long a space of time.

Amleth, Prince of Denmark

After these deeds in Denmark he equipped three vessels lavishly, and went back to Britain to see his wife and her father.

He had also enrolled in his service the flower of the warriors, and arrayed them very choicely, wishing to have everything now magnificently appointed, even as of old he had always worn contemptible gear, and to change all his old devotion to poverty for outlay on luxury.

He also had a shield made for him, whereon the whole series of his exploits, beginning with his earliest youth, was painted in exquisite designs. This he bore as a record of his deeds of prowess, and gained great increase of fame thereby. Here were to be seen depicted the slaying of Horwedil; the fratricide and incest of Feng; the infamous uncle, the whimsical nephew; the shapes of the hooked stakes; the stepfather suspecting, the stepson dissembling; the various temptations offered, and the woman brought to beguile him; the gaping wolf; the finding of the rudder; the passing of the sand; the entering of the wood; the putting of the straw through the gadfly; the warning of the maiden after the escort was eluded. And likewise could be seen the picture of the palace; the queen there with her son; the slaying of the eavesdropper; and how, after being killed, he was boiled down, and so dropped into the sewer, and so thrown out to the swine; how his limbs were strewn in the mud, and so left for the beasts to finish. Also it could be seen how Amleth surprised the secret of his sleeping attendants, how he erased the letters, and put new characters in their places; how he disdained the banquet and scorned the drink; how he condemned the face of the king and taxed the queen with faulty behavior. There was also represented the hanging of the envoys, and the young man's wedding; then the voyage back to Denmark; the festive celebration of the funeral rites.

Amleth, in answer to questions, pointing to the sticks in place of his attendants, acting as cup-bearer, and purposely drawing his sword and pricking his fingers; the sword riveted through, the swelling cheers of the banquet, the dance growing fast and furious; the hangings flung upon the sleepers, then fastened with the interlacing crooks, and wrapped tightly round them as they slumbered; the brand set to the mansion, the burning of the guests, the royal palace consumed with fire and tottering down; the visit to the sleeping-room of Feng, the theft of his sword, the useless one set in its place; and the king slain with his own sword's point by his stepson's hand. All this was there, painted upon Amleth's battle-shield by a careful craftsman in the choicest of handiwork; he copied truth in his figures, and embodied real deeds in his outlines. Moreover, Amleth's

14

followers, to increase the splendor of their presence, wore shields which were gilt over.

The King of Britain received them very graciously, and treated them with costly and royal pomp. During the feast he asked anxiously whether Feng was alive and prosperous. His son−in−law told him that the man of whose welfare he was vainly inquiring had perished by the sword. With a flood of questions he tried to find out who had slain Feng, and learnt that the messenger of his death was likewise its author. And when the king heard this, he was secretly aghast, because he found that an old promise to avenge Feng now devolved upon himself. For Feng and he had determined of old, by a mutual compact, that one of them should act as the avenger of the other.

Thus the king was drawn one way by his love for his daughter and his affection for his son−in−law, another way by his regard for his friend, and moreover by his strict oath and the sanctity of their mutual declarations, which it was impious to violate. At last he slighted the ties of kinship, and sworn faith prevailed. His heart turned to vengeance, and he put the sanctity of his oath before family bonds. But since it was thought sin to wrong the holy ties of hospitality, he preferred to execute his revenge by the hand of another, wishing to mask his secret crime with a show of innocence.

So he veiled his treachery with attentions, and hid his intent to harm under a show of zealous goodwill.

His queen having lately died of illness, he requested Amleth to undertake the mission of making him a fresh match, saying that he was highly delighted with his extraordinary shrewdness. He declared that there was a certain queen reigning in Scotland, whom he vehemently desired to marry. Now he knew that she was not only unwedded by reason of her chastity, but that in the cruelty of her arrogance she had always loathed her wooers, and had inflicted on her lovers the uttermost punishment, so that not one out of all the multitude was to be found who has not paid for his insolence with his life.

Perilous this commission was, Amleth started, never shrinking to obey the duty imposed on him, but trusting partly in his own servants, and partly in the attendants of the king. He entered Scotland, and, when quite close to the abode of the queen, he went into a meadow by the wayside to rest his horses. Pleased by the look of the spot, he thought of resting—the pleasant prattle of the stream exciting a desire to sleep—and posted men to keep watch some way off.

The queen on hearing of this, sent out ten warriors to spy on the approach of the foreigners and their equipment. One of these, being quick–witted, slipped past the sentries, pertinaciously made his way up, and took away the shield, which Amleth had chanced to set at his head before he slept, so gently that he did not ruffle his slumbers, though he was lying upon it, nor awaken one man of all that troop; for he wished to assure his mistress not only by report but by some token. With equal address he filched the letter entrusted to Amleth from the coffer in which it was kept. When these things were brought to the queen, she scanned the shield narrowly, and from the notes appended made out the whole argument. Then she knew that here was the man who, trusting his own nicely–calculated scheme, had avenged on his uncle the murder of his father.

She also looked at the letter containing the suit for her hand, and rubbed out all the writing; for wedlock with the old she utterly abhorred, and desired the embraces of young men. But she wrote in its place a commission purporting to be sent from the King of Britain to herself, signed like the other with his name and title, wherein she pretended that she was asked to marry the bearer. Moreover, she included an account of the deeds of which she had learnt from Amleth's shield, so that one would have thought the shield confirmed the letter, while the letter explained the shield. Then she told the same spies whom she had employed before to take the shield back, and put the letter in its place again; playing the very trick on Amleth which, as she had learnt, he had himself used in outwitting his companions.

Amleth, meanwhile, who found that his shield had been filched from under his head, deliberately shut his eyes and cunningly feigned sleep, hoping to regain by pretended what he had lost by real slumbers. For he thought that the success of his one attempt would incline the spy to deceive him a second time. And he was not mistaken. For as the spy came up stealthily, and wanted to put back the shield and the writing in their old place, Amleth leapt up, seized him, and detained him in bonds. Then he roused his retinue, and went to the abode of the queen. As representing his father–in–law, he greeted her, and handed her the writing, sealed with the king's seal.

The queen who was named Hermutrude, took and read it, and spoke most warmly of Amleth's diligence and shrewdness, saying that Feng had deserved his punishment, and that the unfathomable wit of Amleth had accomplished a deed past all human estimation; seeing that not only had his impenetrable depth devised a mode of revenging his father's death and his mother's adultery, but it had further, by his notable deeds of prowess, seized the kingdom of the man whom he had found constantly plotting against him. She marveled therefore that a man of such instructed mind could have made the one slip of a mistaken marriage; for though his renown almost rose above mortality, he seemed to have stumbled into an obscure and ignoble match. For the parents of his wife had been slaves, though good luck had graced them with the honors of royalty.

Now (said she), when looking for a wife, a wise man must reckon the luster of her birth and not of her beauty. Therefore if he were to seek a match in a proper spirit, he should weigh the ancestry, and not be smitten by the looks; for though looks were a lure to temptation, yet their empty bedizenment had tarnished the white simplicity of many a man.

Now there was a woman, as nobly born as himself, whom he could take. She herself, whose means were not poor nor her birth lowly, was worthy his embraces, since he did not surpass her in royal wealth nor outshine her in the honor of his ancestors. Indeed she was a queen, and but that her sex gainsaid it, might be deemed a king; nay (and this is yet truer), whomsoever she thought worthy of her bed was at once a king, and she yielded her kingdom with herself. Thus her scepter and her hand went together. It was no mean favor for such a woman to offer her love, who in the case of other men had always followed her refusal with the sword. Therefore she pressed him to transfer his wooing, to make over to her his marriage vows, and to learn to prefer birth to beauty. So saying, she fell upon him with a close embrace.

Amleth was overjoyed at the gracious speech of the maiden, fell to kissing back, and returned her close embrace, protesting that the maiden's wish was his own. Then a banquet was held, friends bidden, the chief nobles gathered, and the marriage rites performed. When they were accomplished, he went back to Britain with his bride, a strong band of Scots being told to follow close behind, the he might have its help against the diverse treacheries in his path. As he was returning, the daughter of the King of Britain, to whom he was still married, met him. Though she complained that she was slighted by the wrong of having a paramour put over her, yet, she said, it would be unworthy for her to hate him as an adulterer more than she loved him as a husband; nor would she so far shrink from her lord as to bring herself to hide in silence the guile which she knew was intended against him. For she had a son as a pledge of their marriage, and regard for him, if nothing else, must have inclined his mother to the affection of a wife.

"He", she said, "may hate the supplanter of is mother, I will love her; no disaster shall put out my flame for thee; no ill—will shall quench it, or prevent me from exposing the malignant designs against thee, or from revealing the snares I have detected. Bethink thee, then, that thou must beware of thy father—in—law, for thou hast thyself reaped the harvest of thy mission, foiled the wishes of him who sent thee, and with willful trespass seized over all the fruit for thyself." By this speech she showed herself more inclined to love her husband than her father.

While she thus spoke, the King of Britain came up and embraced his son—in—law closely, but with little love, and welcomed him with a banquet, to hide his intended guile under a show of generosity. But Amleth, having learnt the deceit, dissembled his fear, took a retinue of two hundred horsemen, put on an under—shirt [of mail], and complied with the invitation, preferring the peril of falling in with the king's deceit to the shame of hanging back. So much heed for honor did he think that he must take in all things.

As he rode up close, the king attacked him just under the porch of the folding doors, and would have thrust him through with his javelin, but that the hard shirt of mail threw off the blade. Amleth received a slight wound, and went to the spot where he had bidden the Scottish warriors wait on duty. He then sent back to the king his new wife's spy, whom he had captured. This man was to bear witness that he had secretly taken from the coffer where it was kept the letter which was meant for his mistress, and thus was to make the whole blame recoil on Hermutrude, by this studied excuse absolving Amleth from the charge of treachery.

The king without tarrying pursued Amleth hotly as he fled, and deprived him of his forces. So Amleth, on the morrow, wishing to fight for dear life, and utterly despairing of his powers of resistance, tried to increase his apparent numbers. He put stakes under some of the dead bodies of his comrades to prop them up, set others on horseback like living men, and tied others to neighboring stones, not taking off any of their armor, and dressing them in due order of line and wedge, just as if they were about to engage. The wing composed of the dead was as thick as the troop of the living. It was an amazing spectacle this, of dead men dragged out to battle, and corpses mustered to fight.

The plan served him well, for the very figures of the dead men showed like a vast array as the sunbeams struck them. For those dead and senseless shapes restored the original number of the army so well, that the mass might have been unthinned by the slaughter of yesterday. The Britons, terrified at the spectacle, fled before fighting, conquered by the dead men whom they had overcome in life. I cannot tell whether to think more of the cunning or of the good fortune of this victory The Danes came down on the king as he was tardily making off, and killed him. Amleth, triumphant, made a great plundering, seized the spoils of Britain, and went back with his wives to his own land.

Meanwhile Rorik had died, and Wiglek, who had come to the throne, had harassed Amleth's mother with all manner of insolence and stripped her of her royal wealth, complaining that her son had usurped the kingdom of Jutland and defrauded the King of Leire, who had the sole privilege of giving away and taking away the rights of high offices. This treatment Amleth took with such forbearance as apparently to return kindness for slander, for he presented Wiglek with the riches of his spoils. But afterwards he seized a chance of taking vengeance, attacked him, subdued him, and from a cover became an open foe.

Fialler, the governor of Skanne and Zealand, sent envoys to challenge Amleth to a war. Amleth, with his marvelous shrewdness, saw that he was tossed between two difficulties, one of which involved disgrace and the other danger. For he knew that if he took up the challenge he was threatened with the peril of his life, while to shrink from it would disgrace his reputation as a soldier. Yet in that spirit ever fixed on deeds of prowess the desire to save his honor won the day. Dread of disaster was blunted by more vehement thirst for glory; he would not tarnish the unblemished luster of his fame by timidly skulking from his fate. Also he saw that there is almost as wide a gap between a mean life and a noble death as that which is acknowledged between honor and disgrace themselves.

Yet he was enchained by such love for Hermutrude, that he was more deeply concerned in his mind about her future widowhood than about his own death, and cast about very zealously how he could decide on some second husband for her before the opening of the war. Hermutrude, therefore, declared that she had the courage of a man, and promised that she would not forsake him even on the field, saying that the woman who dreaded to be untied with her lord in death was abominable. But she kept this rare promise ill; for when Amleth had been slain by Wiglek in battle in Jutland, she yielded herself up unasked to be the conqueror's spoil and bride.

Thus all vows of women are loosed by change of fortune and melted by the drifting of time; the faith of their soul rests on a slippery foothold, and is weakened by casual chances; glib in promises, and as sluggish in performance, all manner of lustful promptings enslave it, and it bounds away with panting and precipitate desire, forgetful of old things, in the ever hot pursuit after something.

So ended Amleth. Had fortune been as kind to him as nature, he would have equaled the gods in glory, and surpassed the labors of Hercules by his deeds of prowess. A plain in Jutland is to be found, famous for his name and burial–place.

CPSIA information can be obtained
at www.ICGtesting.com
Printed in the USA
BVHW022315150223
658636BV00019B/247